60 Seconds:

How to tell your company's story & the brain science that makes it stick

By

Andrew Angus

60 Seconds: How to tell your company's story & the brain science that makes it stick.

Andrew Angus

Copyright © 2012
Switch Marketing and Communications Limited

ISBN: 978-1480237599
ISBN Digital: 9781450146662

Published by Switch Publishing
43 Elgin Street
Collingwood, ON L9Y 3L6
www.switchvideo.com

Cover by Switch Video
Printed in the United States of America

DEDICATION

To my mother Barbara and my children Foster and Reed.

Have questions?
Call me on Clarity
clarity.fm/andrewangus

Andrew Angus
📍 San Francisco, CA

Founder / CEO of Switch Video -->
Producer of animated videos that
explain what your company does....
More

| FREE | Request a Call |

Andrew donates to:
charity: water ($47.5)

Don't forget, to get free access to the online course go to
http://learn.switchvideo.com/book
and sign up now!

CONTENTS

Foreword

In the past five years, my company, Switch Video, has helped two hundred fifty businesses and organizations tell the stories about their products and services. We've worked in fourteen different countries for major brands like Microsoft, IBM, HP, Cisco, Unisys, AMEX, the Hong Kong Jockey Club, Salesforce Rypple, the Entrepreneurs Organization, the World Bank, and the United Nations.

Without tooting our own horn (maybe just a short beep), most of our clients not only love the videos we produce and the results they get, but really enjoy working with us, too. How do we know? They've told us so in seven different languages.

I wrote this book to share what I've learned about both the craft and business of storytelling, and to offer some new tools and insights that could help you tell your own company's story to your partners, customers, clients, and employees.

This book takes the process of what it's like to work with Switch Video and turns it into a model anyone can replicate to connect with their target audience and increase sales in the process. It's designed to be easy to read and easy to act on, backed up by the actual research and science behind how and why our approach really works.

If you're a founder, CEO, marketing manager or product manager or someone who wants to utilize and optimize video for their company, come along and take a ride. I promise to make it a fast, fun tour and also get you home on time.

Chapter One: Switching Plans

I'm going to tell you my own story in just 60 seconds (depending on how fast you read).

To give you an idea of how it all began, I started a home heating business, Switch Fuel, a company that would take switch grass, a perennial prairie grain, and compress it into pellets that could be burned in pellet stoves and furnaces.

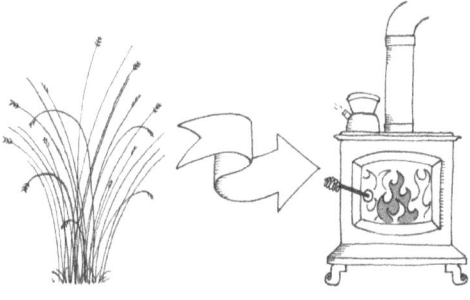

An alternative fuel made from a natural resource. Brilliant idea, right?

But I soon discovered it was hard to get the key selling points across to potential customers and investors. So I figured I'd make a video to explain my story quickly and effectively.

I produced a short PowerPoint presentation, recorded a lo-fi voiceover, and turned it into a video. To put it mildly, it was awful. Based on its quality alone, my idea for a progressive home heating method was sure to go up in smoke.

Then, a funny thing happened.

I put the video up on YouTube and over the next few weeks, five hundred people watched it. Through their direct feedback, I learned things in the next four weeks that would have taken me months without the help of the video.

End of story, right?

Wrong. What I realized was that video is the single most powerful tool you can use to communicate a story— and that this kind of work was what I was actually supposed to be doing.

So I made the switch from the home heating business into video production, a place where I could actually set the world on fire.

And this is where our real story begins.

Chapter Two: Blast Off

Making videos isn't exactly rocket science, especially in a time when anyone with PowerPoint, a microphone and screen capture software can call themselves a producer. But making memorable and impactful videos is another story, and in my company's case, the key to success is *brain science*.

Let me go back before I jump into the intricate workings of the brain. When I first made the jump from Switch Fuel to Switch Video, it wasn't as if I immediately started creating award-winning projects. In fact, some of my first efforts were amateurish and lacked any real production value. Yet, to my surprise, they still seemed to be rather effective and the clients were happy.

I started working on national training programs for the Home Depot and then traveled across Canada, producing (poor-quality!) PowerPoint videos. But we had a great response to these videos and they wildly exceeded our clients' expectations. Even though the videos we produced were still not very polished, they were simple and they were visual. And as it turns out, Home Depot hadn't used video in the past to do these training programs.

Online video is the fastest-growing ad format in 2012 with **nearly 55% growth**.—*eMarketer, January 2012*

What I learned from this experience was *the power of simple storytelling*. That was the real key, and the overall quality of the videos was almost secondary. I know this sounds ass-backwards, especially to anyone in the video production business, but it was true.

I did these kinds of projects for another two years and naturally, the production values improved. Then, I realized I'd built up a skill set and could pivot away from the training side to PR and marketing.

But first, I wanted to know why these fairly basic videos were working so well. So before taking the next step, I went back and talked to my mother, who's a cognitive psychologist.

I asked her to explain to me why these videos I was producing were so simple but were getting good—no, actually great—results.

She explained to me the three keys of brain science, as they applied to making successful videos:

1. Keep the story simple.

2. Connect with people's prior knowledge.

3. Stimulate both the auditory and visual senses.

Thus, I had a foundation for the next stage of our business: PR and marketing. Now that I was aware of the underlying brain science, I designed a process for producing videos for our clients that would incorporate each of the basic principles of in all of our work.

Once this process was in place, our company started growing exponentially. And we've produced more than three hundred fifty videos for our clients.

I don't know if it was genetics or osmosis, but I owe a big thanks to my mom because as it turns out, brain science may not be rocket science, but it definitely helped Switch Video take off.

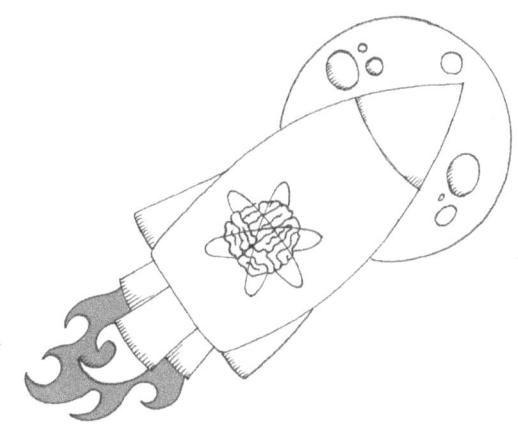

Chapter Three: Check the Pipes

Since the goal of this book is to teach you how to tell a story in just one minute, I'm not going to get into all the nuances of brain science, but instead, try to put it into simple, concise concepts that directly relate to making videos. That said, I still need to lay a little groundwork.

People have been telling stories for many thousands of years and believe it or not, some of the things that were effective way back when are just as powerful today. Yes, early explorers, historians, marketers, salesmen and women didn't have digital cameras, computer graphics, audio software and non-linear editing, but through trial and error, they found out what worked. While they didn't know they were utilizing some of the basic principles of brain science, templates of those same stories have been passed down from generation to generation.

But unlike the hit-and-miss method of yesteryear, now we know how the brain actually works and can create

Video and other multimedia product viewing options were rated **more effective than any other site initiatives** in an Adobe survey of almost 2,000 interactive marketers.—*Adobe* videos to take full advantage of this intelligence.

The first step is always to *keep things simple*. The reason for this is that whoever is watching and listening to a story is using what we call working memory to make meaning out of it. You only have so much space for incoming information and this new information has to connect your working memory (the present) to your long-term memory (the past) to be able to process and retain it.

But you need to have the incoming information come through at just the right rate, so that your long-term memory will be stimulated and accessed, but the working memory isn't overwhelmed with too much new data and detail. Once there is synchronization, this creates a whole new set of information that now gets sent off for long-term storage. So new information meets old memories, they join up and create *new* old memories.

Stay with me, it gets better.

Again, if you have too many ideas coming into working memory too quickly, you can't process them all or remember them. Or you're processing one idea and getting into long-term memory, but then you're missing idea two, three, four, or five. So you have to be really careful to keep your core message simple and give people enough time to do the intricate elaborations and processes that connect working memory to long-term memory.

The other idea is that your brain has a certain capacity. Think of it as a watertight vessel with only so much space in it and the new information as a jug of water. We're going to take that new information and pour it into the working memory.

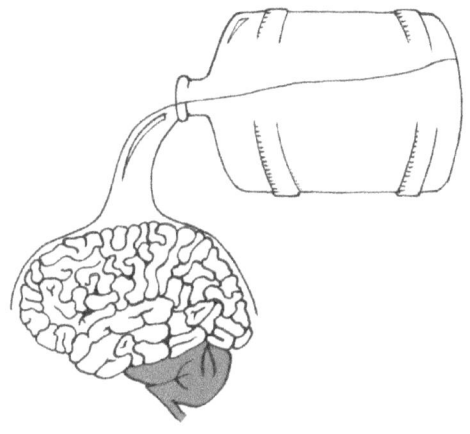

If there's more information in your jug of water than there is space in your working memory, then you have the water flowing over the sides. What that means is that you're losing content from the message that you're trying to tell about your company.

While we're pouring in this new information, imagine a tube at the bottom that is also moving some of the water in the vessel into a container, your long-term memory. And it's not that you have to stop pouring, but just do it at the right rate, so there's a balanced flow between the incoming ideas and outgoing storage.

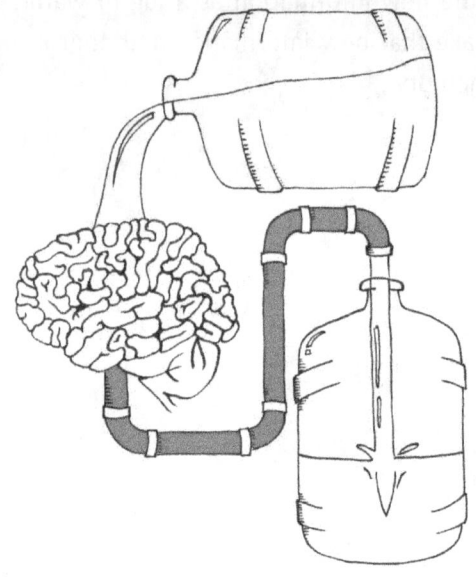

But it's not only size and rate involved in the brain's hydraulic system. It's about combining the written or spoken word with visual images to create a hybrid form of intra-communication called *visual language*.

In a paper prepared for the National Science Foundation Conference on Converging Technologies for Improving Human Performance, Stanford University visiting scholar Robert E. Horn talks about the impact of visual language.

"Today, human beings work and think in fragmented ways, but visual language has the potential to integrate our existing skills to make them tremendously more effective. With support from developments in information technology, visual language has the potential for increasing human "bandwidth," the capacity to take in, comprehend, and more efficiently synthesize large amounts of new information."

"The deep understanding of the patterns of visual language will permit:"

- More rapid, more effective interdisciplinary communication

- More complex thinking, leading to a new era of thought

- Facilitation of business, government, scientific, and technical productivity

- Potential breakthroughs in education and training productivity

- Greater efficiency and effectiveness in all areas of knowledge production and distribution

- Better cross-cultural communication

Speaking of bandwidth, Switch has always focused on creating really simple illustrations because when you're doing crazy 3-D animations, you're often filling the working memory with information that isn't necessary, and can often be a distraction from the core of the real story you're trying to tell.

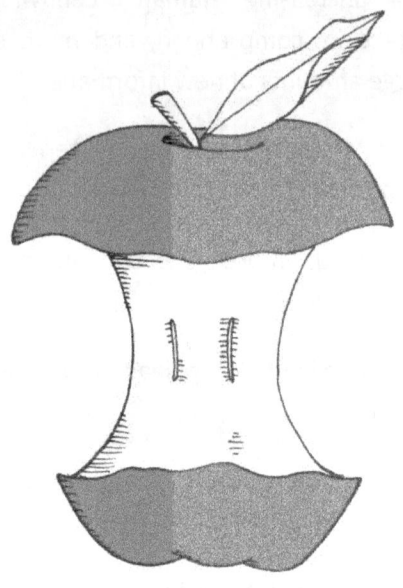

While I appreciate great design and animation (and we have a killer team of animators and artists at Switch), if you're filling the brain with the dazzling visuals just to show off how technically skilled you are, that's doesn't help your client explain what it is their company actually does, and won't help the person watching the video retain the messaging and information.

People tell stories to convey things that are important to them. In a business context, people tell their stories to influence decision makers or consumers to purchase their product or service**.**

The bottom line in visual language is finding that magic equilibrium between working and long-term memory. And as the saying goes, less really can be more.

People who view a web video are 64% more likely to purchase than other site visitors.—*Comscore*

Chapter Four: The Clock is Ticking

In today's accelerated digital universe, time and language are being compressed at unprecedented rates. When conducting business, many people avoid meetings or phone calls because they take away too much time from their schedules. Some opt to communicate strictly via e-mail and others prefer texting. Clearly, shorter is better.

We have people contact us all the time about creating a video and they say, "Oh, you couldn't possibly tell the story of our company in 60 or 90 seconds. It will take at least five minutes."

Well, the truth is people are not going to watch a five-minute video and even if they do, it's highly unlikely they're really absorbing and retaining the information.

What you have to realize is that your story has to solve someone else's problem, and you have to come up with a way of expressing that concisely. One way to do that is to chunk the story into simple metaphors, so you're connecting to knowledge people already have.

Here's a simple, but appropriate example. Let's say you have business that enables dog owners to meet other dog owners so their dogs can play together.

You go on to explain all the benefits of having two dogs interact and exercise together. You go into detail about how schedules can be matched up. Then, you talk about why the dogs also have to be well-suited to each other by size, breed, temperament, etc.

Finally, you list all the reasons why your company does this better than anyone else's.

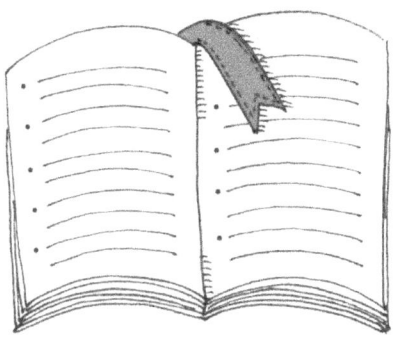

A better way to communicate this story would be to say your service is like eHarmony for dogs. Most people already know what eHarmony is, so you can immediately tap into their long-term memory. Everyone knows what a dating service is and suddenly, you've already cut most of your story down to a sentence or two.

A metaphor effectively distills a lot of incoming information and makes it easier for someone to connect it with prior knowledge. Once you have established this link, the more meaningful the connections are and the more accessible they will be later.

At Switch, we spend a lot of time creating metaphors in our videos because they're so powerful. A strong metaphor activates large areas of memory quickly and that's what you want, because if you don't connect the incoming information (working memory) with the viewer's long-term memory in the first five to ten seconds, it's lost.

> Time spent watching video ads totaled
> **3.9 billion minutes**.

It's also critical to know your audience, to ensure they will understand the metaphors you're employing. If you're not talking about something in a way they will easily grasp, you've lost them.

> Retail site visitors who view video stay
> **two minutes longer** on average.—*Comscore*

Chapter Five: Dollars and Senses

Why is video the best way to tell a story? Video is the optimal form of communicating information because when you stimulate the auditory and visual senses at the same time, a viewer's retention rate greatly increases.

When you read or listen to something, you're stimulating the auditory sense. Studies show that if you only stimulate the auditory sense, people retain just 10% of that information. But when you stimulate both the auditory and the visual senses, you end up with a retention rate of 68%. This involves the *dual-coding theory*.

Dual-coding theory refers to what happens when you simultaneously receive information verbally and visually. Information you receive verbally is coded in one way and information you receive visually is coded in another. So to have both acting together allows for a person to really comprehend what he or she is being shown. If someone is a more visual learner, the images are necessary to help him or her understand information. If someone is a more auditory learner, then the words support the images. With dual coding, everyone is catered to specifically, and in the best way possible.

The verbal information is processed sequentially, so that each word has a representation for a meaning.

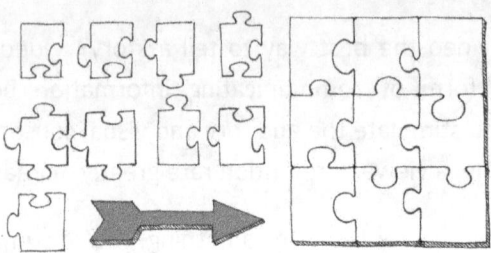

When you support the auditory channel with a visual, more details that can be stored away in memory because rather than being sequential, the image is more holistic.

That's why video, and especially animated video, is so effective. (It's important to note that having a head speaking to the camera is not necessarily dual coding, because in that case, the video would only be stimulating the auditory sense.)

So you've got two memory traces, with two different kinds of coding, which means there are more paths leading to the memory.

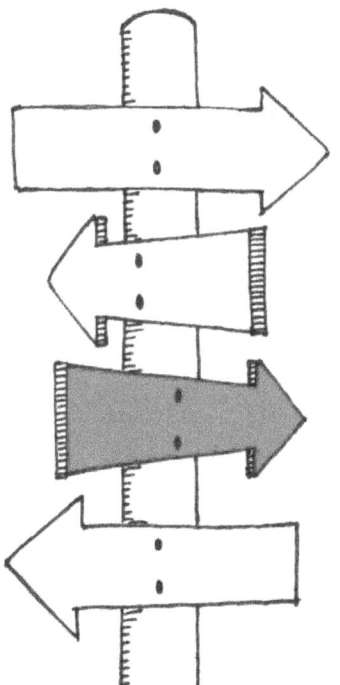

Having memories is one thing, but being able to retrieve them is actually the important part. You have to be able to go in and find where the information is stored, so the more entry points, the better.

In a 60-second story, we want to combine audio and visual metaphors to not only reduce the amount of time it takes to tell the story, but to activate more long-term memory. When people retain information longer about who you are, what you do, and what benefits you have to offer, they are more likely to visit your website, click on a link, send you an e-mail, or call you.

Retail site visitors who view video stay **two minutes longer** on average and are **64% more likely to purchase** than other site visitors.—*Comscore, August 2010*

Chapter Six: Second That Emotion

Stories are powerful tools for making personal connections and helping people align with other people. It's the human element, relationship building.

As a consumer, while you're doing your research and deciding whether to purchase item A, B, or C, you're using the cognitive part of your brain.

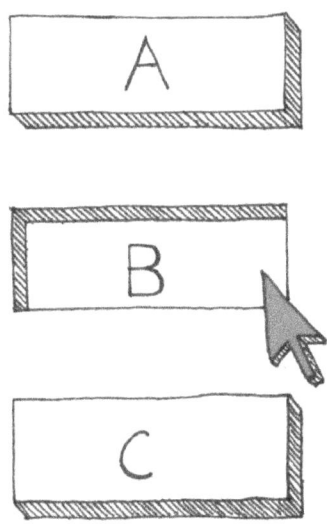

You're thinking about the advantages of one versus the other. So you've created a mental chart of the positives and negatives as you sift through options.

But when it comes down to actually making your choices, then, the emotional part of your brain kicks in and we know that making a personal/emotional connection drives the final decision, even though you've spent all that other time doing cognitive analysis.

What's interesting about our process is people often ask about what the ROI will be on their video, how it will directly translate into sales, as if that's the real barometer of a successful video. But when they see their final video, they understand that the goal is to first create a personal connection to the story. So rather than just being offered factual information, we're inviting the viewer to become emotionally invested.

Once that investment has been made, then you're really on the road to ROI.

> According to *Internet Retailer*, **52% of consumers say that watching product videos makes them more confident in their online purchase decisions**. When a video is information-intensive, **66% of consumers** will watch the video two or more times.—*Internet Retailer (2012)*

Chapter Seven: How We Do It

Okay, it's time to move from the scientific theories and see exactly how these tools and practices apply to our work.

One of the best examples is the video we made for Salesforce. Rypple is a web-based social performance management platform that helps companies improve performance through social goals, continuous feedback, and meaningful recognition.

Whoa! Wait a minute! Is your brain already struggling to match those words to your own familiar long-term memories? Not to worry: we'll find that special balance between long- and short-term memory that we discussed earlier.

After being acquired by Salesforce, Rypple wanted to make a video that was less about what their software does to improve performance reviews in a corporate setting, but instead, get visitors to their site to emotionally connect to the feeling of being disengaged and unsatisfied in their day-to-day jobs, and their relationships with their managers. Unfortunately, this probably sounds familiar to some of you.

This was one of the first cases where we learned to really focus on the problem and getting the viewer to tap into their emotions. Rather than an 'explainer' video, where we would spend maybe a third of the time on the set-up/problem and two thirds on the solution, we did the opposite, so less than a third of the script was spent on the actual solution.

As a client, Rypple pushed us in new directions because they realized that by getting people to think, "Oh yeah, I know that feeling," they would go deeper into their site to find out more. Plus, as Rypple's product continued to evolve, they wouldn't have to keep updating the video.

Rather than offer a typical value proposition, the video doesn't go into detail of how Rypple works. Instead, it alludes to the fact that there is this antiquated style of management that basically sucks (we actually used the word 'suck' in the script) and that there's a better way to do things.

First, this is the written script for the finished piece.

Meet Jessica. Jessica loves her job.

But lately, she's stressed. She wonders if she's focused on the right stuff. Does her team appreciate her work?

Jess is hungry for feedback. It's hard to stay engaged when you don't know where you stand.

Meanwhile, Mike, Jessica's manager, is feeling underwater. He wants his team to do well, but it takes more time than he's got to stay on top of what everyone's doing.

It's hard to balance coaching his team with getting his own work done.

To make things worse, annual performance reviews are around the corner and they suck. It's like they're from another century. The feedback is too little, too late, and everyone thinks the whole process is a huge waste of time.

What's wrong with this picture? Why are great people like Jessica and Mike feeling stressed and disconnected?

Lack of recognition, feedback, and coaching. Time-consuming processes that don't make sense anymore.

Mike wonders why in a real-time world, people struggle to get real-time feedback and coaching.

There has to be a better way.

What if it were fast and easy to have meaningful one-on-ones?

What if it was fun to give feedback and stay connected?

What if teams stayed on track and people felt valued?

Imagine modern social software that changes the way you work.

Imagine your team inspired and learning all the time. Imagine always being on the right track.

Don't imagine anymore. Make it real.

Sign your team up to Rypple today.

That all made sense, didn't' it? But did it really stir your emotions? Now, check out the images we also used to tell the story

Meet Jessica. Jessica loves her job.

But lately, she's stressed. She wonders if she's focused on the right stuff. Does her team appreciate her work? Jess is hungry for feedback. It's hard to stay engaged when you don't know where you stand.

Meanwhile, Mike, Jessica's manager, is feeling underwater.

He wants his team to do well, but it takes more time than he's got to stay on top of what everyone's doing.

It's hard to balance coaching his team with getting his own work done.

To make things worse, annual performance reviews are around the corner and they suck. It's like they're from another century.

The feedback is too little, too late, and everyone thinks the whole process is a huge waste of time.

What's wrong with this picture? Why are great people like Jessica and Mike feeling stressed and disconnected?

Lack of recognition, feedback, and coaching. Time-consuming processes that don't make sense anymore.

Mike wonders why in a real-time world, people struggle to get real-time feedback and coaching.

There has to be a better way.

What if it were fast and easy to have meaningful one-on-ones?

What if it was fun to give feedback and stay connected?

What if teams stayed on track and people felt valued?

Imagine modern social software that changes the way you work.

Imagine your team inspired and learning all the time. Imagine always being on the right track.

Don't imagine anymore. Make it real.

Sign your team up to Rypple today.

Here's the basic formula we followed to make the video work:

- Keep the story simple

- Connect with peoples prior knowledge

- Use metaphors

- Stimulate the auditory and visual senses

Of course, one of the big tradeoffs of writing a book about video is that the reader can't see how the images animate, or hear the music and voice tracks. That's where the real magic kicks in.

If you're near any digital device with web access right now, please go to
http://www.switchvideo.com/portfolio/rypple to watch the Rypple video. Go ahead, I'll wait.

According to our client, the general comment Rypple gets from people who watch the video is, "I'm not entirely sure what this product is, but I know I know I need it at my work." They want it because they feel Jessica's pain and they feel her manager, Mike's, pain.

They click at the end to sign up for the free trial and our case study shows that after introducing this video on their web site, Rypple's conversion rate increased by 20%.

Why was the video so successful? We just let people know that Rypple felt their pain!

59% of senior executives prefer to watch video instead of reading text, if both are available on the same page. **80% of executives are watching more online video today than they were a year ago.** - *Forbes Insight, December 2010*

Chapter Eight: Trust the Process

The three promises that we make to our clients are critical for all of our interactions internally as a team, as well as externally with our clients. I developed these three promises after being frustrated with other companies' customer service. If you spend some time with me, you'll undoubtedly hear me talking about customer service and why ours has to be better than our competitors'.

First, we set reasonable expectations and promise we'll meet them (and we don't promise what we can't deliver). The second is that we'll complete all aspects of the job and you won't have to ask us twice to do something. Third is that we'll keep you informed every step of the way, so that you know where your project is and the status of any changes and deadlines.

In conjunction with those three promises, we also adhere to a strict five-step productions process. We've built the foundation of this company on these promises and our process. It's the most important thing that we do every day.

At Switch, we take every client through the same process from start to finish. Ideally, this progression will start and finish in five weeks.

Before I explain these steps in detail, it's important to note that before we begin any new project, our clients need to agree to our production process in writing. We've learned that buy-in is an absolutely essential element in every successful project.

We also ask them to commit to using web-based tools like Google Docs, Basecamp, and Proof HQ, so that things keep moving forward smoothly and efficiently.

With today's assortment of devices and platforms to share information and images, clients should be able to access anything, any time. So it doesn't matter whether you're on a desktop, laptop, tablet, or Smartphone, we'll make sure we're connected. And that includes whatever language you need to speak to your audience in.

It's all part of the service.

76% of marketers plan to add video to their sites in 2012, making it a higher priority than Facebook, Twitter, and blog integration.
—*Social Media Examiner, April 2012*

Chapter Nine: Meeting of the Minds

Step One: DISCOVERY

The *Discovery* phase is vitally important. That's where we want to get our team and everyone in our client's company on the same page. Sometimes, a client will want to skip this step and think, "Oh, I'm the decision maker. I can be in charge of discovery and lay the foundation for this project. Then, I'll just keep checking in with the production team and we'll produce this awesome video that I can show to my bosses and they'll think I'm incredible." That's usually a blueprint for disaster.

Discovery is about defining who the key decision makers are and making sure they're already at the table. Your company's story is incredibly important; it's what your employees tell potential clients or customers and it's what your existing clients and customers tell other people. To build a solid foundation for your video project, you must have the right stakeholders at the table from the start.

If you're a small company of twenty or thirty people and there's a founder of the company, that founder better be at the table. If you're a larger company, you want to make sure that your boss's boss is aware of what's going on, so that you don't get to the end of the process, having invested a considerable amount of time, energy, and money, and find out that while you told a great story in the video, it was the wrong one.

We have a survey that all of our clients take when we start. That survey becomes the reference document for the discovery process. It poses questions such as:

- What would you like this video to explain?

- What is your company's elevator pitch?

- Who is the target audience of your video?

- What is the one key message that you would like each viewer to remember after watching this video?

For more information, feel free to check out ***www.switchvideo.com/book/discovery.***

After it's completed, we have a meeting with everyone and get some buy-in about the discovery survey. Then, we ask the client to take the resulting creative brief to his or her boss and get them to sign off on it—and we mean to literally sign the document. When people sign their name to something, they're more likely to be invested in that project.

Just like any good relationship, we're looking for good communication and a firm commitment. And when in doubt, a little chocolate never hurts, either.

Once we've finished the Discovery phase, we move on to step two.

In a keynote address at CES, YouTube's
Vice President of Global Content Robert Kyncl
said that video would soon be
90% of Internet traffic.—*Forbes (2012)*

Chapter Ten: The Write Stuff

Step Two: SCRIPT

When looking at different mediums of creative broadcast arts, and this applies to everything from online video to broadcast television to feature films, there's one thing for certain. It doesn't matter how much money you spend, how great the talent and visual effects are, or how you decide to market your project, unless you've got one critical element first. A good script. Great storytelling starts with great writing and if you don't have a good script to start with, the rest won't really matter.

Just think about the ads, videos, TV shows, and films you really like and guess what they all have in common. Someone wrote (and rewrote) a script that touched your memories and emotions. It's just as true for the movie that wins the Oscar for best picture as it is for a short video that tells your company's story.

Your script needs to pinpoint the problem or need the consumer has, but you don't reach people on an emotional level by trying to sell them something. You do it by *making them feel like you understand their issues and desires*. You need to speak to them personally, not just professionally. Too many companies get caught up in sell, sell, sell, when the real ROI comes from tell, tell, tell.

Tell an accessible story, one the customer can easily relate to. We've been very effective at helping clients take businesses that seem very complex, and making them very simple.

If you're selling a product, another thing you definitely don't want to do is let the engineer or designer that developed it to make a video about its value and benefits. (No offense to engineers or designers: you are key players in a company's success, but you ain't writers.)

When an engineer or designer thinks about a product, they get excited about all of the incredible features they've created. One of the things we've learned is that the features you think are important aren't necessarily important to the people who use your product. It's not that the features don't matter, because they do, but what people really want is for you to help overcome their challenges and solve their problems. Once you've established this trust in words, you can move on to the next step, the visuals.

When our writers are working on a script, they're constantly thinking about visuals, as well. There's a delicate balance between professionals trained in the art of written and verbal language and those that rely on visual images. But when they both go in knowing the basics of brain science, it makes for an easier and more effective collaboration.

Scriptwriters are constantly rethinking and rewriting, while animators react more instinctively because that's what they're trained to do in visual literacy. But as long as they're both thinking about blending their creative skills with brain science, there's a convergence.

Some people call this dynamic "co-intelligence," where various individuals come together to bring out the best in each other and produce a level of quality that could only be accomplished as a team.

Time spent watching video ads totaled
3.9 billion minutes.

Chapter Eleven: Every Picture Tells a Story

Step Three: STORYBOARD

When it comes to visuals and animation, one challenge we often have with a client, especially a new client, is that we're creative production team and they're businesspeople, and at times, it's almost like we're speaking two different languages. So while we're talking about brain science and why we need to keep the video simple, they may be more focused on including lots of details about the product or service, rather than thinking like we do about a key aspect of the video that's leading the eye and how much information we're asking the viewer to digest or process.

Switch is always focused on really simple illustrations because if you're doing crazy 3-D animations, you're filling the working memory with information that isn't necessary to communicate the basic story. Yes, animators can show how technically skilled they are, but if the visuals don't help the person watching the video grasp and retain what it is the company does, then the images are not of value.

On one project we were working on, our designer felt the best way to lead the eye was to use warm colors. They're very simple and our eyes are just attracted to them. But the client came back and said "No, everything needs to be masculine. Most of our clients will be men. We need this to be much darker." So we also have to balance the client's feedback with the brain science side of it.

There's another effective creative dynamic we've discovered. When we're using humor in the visual, we'll work from a straighter script and if we're using a lot of humor in the script, we'll deliver a straighter visual. That means we're giving the viewer options and delivering key information in a different ways at the same time. With humor (and we like to employ a little wit whenever possible), most people are open to at least a light touch, but we also don't want to lose the ones who either don't really get it or simply want to know the facts.

When you're doing this process on your own internally, it's almost like a closed loop, no matter how creative you think you're being. So we have to get feedback not only from our clients, but their customers, people on the street, even your friends and family. Just tell people your story and see the kind of feedback they give.

Of course, the feedback will vary from different audiences, depending on people's budgets, backgrounds, experiences, and prior knowledge (as well as where they live). But it's very important to determine which feedback will help improve your client's story, so focus on the verticals and demographics that are most likely to use their products or services and use language specific to those verticals. You want feedback from people who are similar to your past clients or likely to be future clients, because those are the ones that your story needs to resonate with.

Americans viewed **9.6 billion video ads in July**, representing another month of record video ad views.

Chapter Twelve: Feed It Forward, Feed It Back

Step Four: *ANIMATION REVIEW*

When we work with clients, the most essential step in our process is the continuing exchange of feedback: whether to hone down the script or change some of the messaging, or to rethink and refine the visuals.

If a client has a very clear, creative idea going in and can communicate it effectively to us, that's great. But sometimes, it's more of a struggle to get it out of them. We often need to teach our clients how to speak to us in creative language, especially when it comes to visuals. We do this by showing them different examples and asking, "Exactly what is it about this that you like or dislike?" And that dialogue keeps happening throughout the entire process.

In some cases, we're basically giving our clients a crash course in video production, as well as a primer on brain science, which is not always the most efficient way to work when it comes to time. But it is the most effective in the long run because an educated client is always the best client.

As our company continues to evolve, some of the most incisive and compelling feedback we've heard from our clients is, "Push back on us more through the process and tell us when we're wrong." That's a really tricky thing to do and it's often hard telling someone that's paying a lot of money for a video that you disagree with his or her ideas. But when the work keeps improving, you build a sense of trust, knowing you're both pursuing the same goal.

The way we keep script and visuals together is through ongoing brainstorming sessions, so at different intervals in projects we meet with a small team of two to four people to discuss the relationship between the visuals and the script. And we have a very intimate office environment. Everyone's just a stone's throw from everybody else, which makes the collaborative work going on in the production studio much more fluid.

We did a fundraising video for the Collingwood General Marine Hospital Foundation that demonstrates how the animation review unfolds. This project is a great example of combining video with brain science.

In Canada, people assume that everything in our healthcare system is publicly funded because they aren't presented with a bill at the end of their treatment.

But it turns out that hospitals have to rely on private donations in order to provide a lot of the equipment and services they have. For example, national healthcare funding does not cover seventy percent of the equipment used in emergency rooms.

So we set out to show what it would be like if you visited an emergency room that only offered the remaining thirty percent.

The executive director of the Collingwood General Marine Hospital Foundation had been telling that same story for twenty-three years and it was only when it was turned into a video that the message actually resonated with potential donors. She's told us it's made their fund-raising efforts so much more successful.

They had a great story. It just needed a transfusion.

A majority of businesspeople surveyed by Forbes in October 2010 said they watched more video currently compared to last year. Virtually **60% of respondents said they would watch video previous to reading text** on the same web page, and **22% said they generally liked watching video more than browsing text** for examining business information.— *eMarketer.com*

Chapter Thirteen:
Independent Do-ers

I'm a chronic entrepreneur. It's just in my blood to start businesses and grow them. But I believe that there are certain basic skills and attributes you need to start and maintain your own business and if you don't have them, I don't necessarily recommend taking the plunge.

To give you an analogy, I play ice hockey and I'm a goaltender. One of the keys to this position is to keep visualizing the game in front of you. It's the same approach I take to running a company and being a CEO.

As a goaltender, you're an incredibly important member of the team. You play the whole game, not just in shifts, where you get some time off on the bench. While you're not skating up and down the ice, you are constantly on alert, seeing how the game plays out and making sure you're ready for the time when you're called upon to make a stop. The action is fast and furious, so and you always have to be ready to react because things can change in an instant and you have to make critical decisions and adjustments.

Before even taking the ice, I always try to visualize the entire game, the types of saves I might have to make and the different scenarios that could play out. I know I'll have to be prepared for whatever might happen. As I go through this whole process, it's really the same thing I do as a CEO. There are all these things happening in the office, players on my team, and the opponents are in constant motion and things keep changing. And I'm sitting back here watching the action in front of me, seeing how things are developing and trying to anticipate what will happen next.

This is also the perfect business for an entrepreneur to help other entrepreneurs follow their dreams, to take their ideas and passions and help them grow and leverage them into dynamic new businesses the world hasn't seen before. I feel so blessed my company can be a part of helping other entrepreneurs create businesses.

All you have to do is drop the puck, start up the ice, and keep your eye on the goal.

The eTailing Group found that 73% of online retailers used video on product pages in 2010, up from 55% in 2009 and only 20% in 2005. 74% of the top 50 retailers used product videos, 40% used category videos, and 38% used other types of informational videos.—*eMarketer, February 2011*

Chapter Fourteen: Crossing the Border

I'm from Canada, which some people in the US think of as a foreign country (and others more like an American province). I find that living here gives me a unique perspective on this business, as our company is in the mainstream of global enterprise, but also not stuck in a cultural mindset. Plus, our offices are in a small town in Southern Ontario, which helps keep us healthy and sane in a frenetic digital universe, which we're very much a part of.

I spend a lot of my time in San Francisco and Silicon Valley and was introduced to an organization called the C100, a non-profit run by successful Canadian entrepreneurs in the valley. Their mission is basically to introduce the most successful Canadian entrepreneurs living in Canada to the most successful Canadian entrepreneurs living in the valley. It's a great organization and we wanted to help them out, so we produced a video for them and they've helped make introductions for us.

1% of the Canadian population lives in the Bay Area and our video has led to a lot of business for us and a lot of goodwill, as it plays before all their events, including for large companies like Google, SAP, and Mozilla.

C100 wanted something light and funny to fire up a crowd and create brand recognition for the organization and drive visitors to their website. Since many of the attendees are obviously from Canada, the video plays on the differences between Canadians and Americans, having a little fun at the expense of both nations. Canadians are delighted to make jokes about beer, hockey, and beavers.

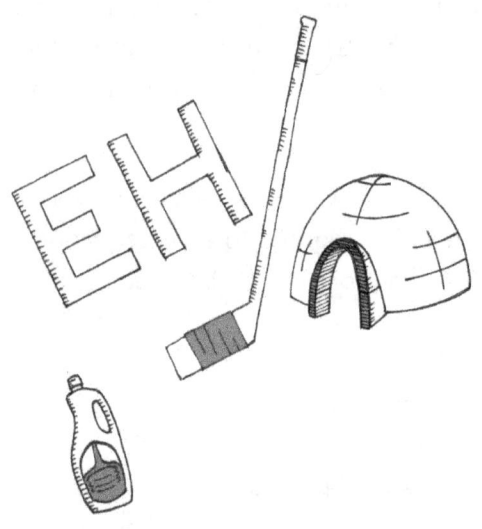

This gave us the opportunity to tell a story that was simple, funny, and easy for everyone to access and process, even after a couple of beers.

It's really inspiring to see our fellow Canadians do so well on an international stage and I'm very proud that the incredible team we've built at Switch is a part of helping some of Canada's most successful entrepreneurs take off in their new ventures.

So a beaver and a bald eagle walk into a bar...

Chapter Fifteen: Just Give Me A Minute

I wrote this book for companies that need to communicate with their customers and consumers and tell truly compelling stories about their products and services. And the best way I can do that is by sharing what I've learned about utilizing video and brain science to optimize this dialogue.

Our overall direction at Switch is to help our clients grow their businesses so they're able to compete locally and globally. In a rapidly changing economic landscape, companies are being presented with all kinds of new challenges and we can either view these developments as scary or exciting, and I greatly prefer the latter.

My goal in sharing our experience and know how is to turn it into a model anyone can replicate to help them connect more effectively with their customers and increase sales in the process. The idea was make this easy to read, easy to act on, and backed up with real science and whenever possible, a little levity. We've found that humor goes a long way in the business world, as both our working and long-term memories love a good chuckle.

Lastly, I want to give a shout-out to all of you entrepreneurs out there. I feel your optimism and passion and believe that the future will be built upon people with new ideas and dreams and a burning desire to fulfill them. I, too, am a chronic entrepreneur, much to my mother's chagrin.

Well, that's my Sixty Seconds (at least, for now). I can't wait to hear your story.

Have questions?
Call me on Clarity
clarity.fm/andrewangus

Andrew Angus
♀ San Francisco, CA

Founder / CEO of Switch Video -->
Producer of animated videos that
explain what your company does....
More

FREE | Request a Call

Andrew donates to:
charity: water ($47.5)

powered by *Clarity*